Tanzania Journal

Tanzania Journal

2023-2024

바른북스

HEEWON SEO

Contents

The Day-10 ⋯ 6

The Day-8 ⋯ 9

The Day-5 ⋯ 11

The Day-3 ⋯ 14

The Day-1 ⋯ 16

D-Day ⋯ 22

Day 1 ⋯ 26

Day 2 ⋯ 33

Day 3 ⋯ 44

Day 4 ⋯ 56

Day 5 ⋯ 64

Day 6 ⋯ 72

Day 7 ⋯ 76

Day 8 ⋯ 79

Day 9 ⋯ 86

Day 10 ⋯ 90

Day 11 ⋯ 99

As I wrap up this trip ⋯ 107

The Day-10

. . . .

My semester got finally over. Now, I really had only a week before my flight, but I still felt like I have about 3 months until departure. I did not want to spend my day meaninglessly since I have fewer break days than other friends staying in Korea. I thought about what could make my trip to Tanzania worth more. Then, I remembered my school's vice principal explaining our school's last trip to Tanzania. He said students who went there could not bear to give children living there everything they had at that time. He said there was even a student who gave his soccer shoes to a child who was bare-foot. My recalling of VP words gave me an idea. I thought it would be so meaningful to prepare Tanzanian students' gifts by myself. I wanted to share this worthwhile opportunity with my boyfriend, Eric, so I shared this idea with him right after the idea popped up in my head. After a short discussion, we decided that it would be even more worthwhile to share this opportunity with all of our friends. That's how Eric and I gathered the 9th graders to plan goody bags. I believed gathering everyone's opinions of what should goody bags have and funding this project with our pocket money were significant since we had to show our dedication. Eric said he want to put Korean candy in it since he wished for them to try Korean culture. John said it would be great to put up a light bulb to help when they study. I could also see some students doing research for this. Their deep consideration made me proud to pitch this idea. I would agree that packing 120 students' gifts was time-consuming and demanding work to do. Nevertheless, I was glad to spend my time like this rather than going over Instagram posts without a single thought going through my head. I cannot bear to see the faces of the children when they receive the gifts. Also, I wonder what I will feel when I hand out those presents. Would I feel proud? Or nothing? Well, maybe I would be somber looking at how much they appreciate things that we could easily get in our daily lives.

The Day-8

. . . .

Christmas ended, which meant it was really time to start my preparation. I did not have to make a list for my package because I already had one. Right after my decision to go to Tanzania was made, I already made a list due to my overflowing excitement during midterm week. It was funny how everything seemed so fun during exam week, even though it was only making a page of a list. Since I already had a list for my package, I wrote out the things I have to do physically before I leave. The most crucial thing to do after getting my body checked was to get all my devices checked. I was planning to bring my phone and laptop to Tanzania.

Someone is probably saying it is an unnecessary process, and I am overreacting. I would rely on saying better than nothing. I did not want my devices to have problems during my major trip. Also, I did not want to disappoint my parents by not being able to handle my belongings safely. Caring for those small details and my stuff made me feel like growing up. I could easily feel that I was getting more responsible for what I had. Fortunately, there was nothing wrong with my devices. I just bought a charger for better, more stable charging for my laptop and reported my process to my parents. I could also notice my parents relief from me being able to think through and control the things I needed. I like how all the processes for my trip make me grow and be proud at the same time. I cannot wait to feel grown up through learning lessons there.

The Day-5

. . . .

I still cannot feel that I have only 5 days left until my flight leaves. Today, I wanted to make another great memory that my parents can remember when I am gone, so I suggested we watch a movie together at night. My mom was absent, but spending the night with my father was another fabulous option for me. I always like driving with my dad. It was because I could learn a lot of things from my dad through conversation. This time too, our driving on the way to the movie theater was remarkable. I gazed at thousands of lights sparkling at night. I felt some overwhelming feelings that I cannot explain. The night in Seoul made me imagine the night in Africa. How would it be? For sure, the darkness will be full of real stars instead of the lights of buildings in Seoul. I feel calm and composed when I stare at the sky at night in Seoul. What would I feel there when I looked up at the sky? Would I be amazed or overwhelmed? Perhaps I am afraid of the amazement of nature I have never seen. I barely remember what I talked about with my dad, but I can still feel the mood and my feelings at that time. I felt safe and warm. I will miss these feelings when I am away from my family. I can also barely recall what the movie was about. To be honest, I kind of fell asleep due to my tiredness. However, it is enough to give my father the memory of his daughter. I am getting old, and I will leave my family when I become an adult. I would consider this trip a practice of leaving each other for my parents and for me. I would consider today's memory as something that can help me to endure my loneliness and something that can aid my parents to overcome how much they miss me when we are apart.

The Day-3

· · · · · · ·

Today was the time to say goodbye to my other family members. Some people will say it is overreacting since it is only a 2-week trip. However, I understand how much my family can be concerned about me going somewhere that takes a day to go and somewhere that they have never heard of. Therefore, our family ended up having lunch with my grandparents. Out of everyone, I thought my grandparents would not agree to send me to Tanzania since they are more unaware of this place. Nevertheless, I underestimated them. They seemed worried, but they encouraged me more. They wanted me to learn more things that I could not learn here. They did not want to hold me back due to any concerns or fears. I love how they respected my decisions. This is the reason why I respect my whole family. Also, this is the reason why I want to grow old like them. Their encouragement made me sure to make up my mind to learn and feel more when I got there. Even though they support me, I made sure to relieve them by telling them how much safer I will be if I am around my teachers. I will make sure to connect with my grandparents sufficiently when I get there. Also, I should not forget to buy souvenirs as proof of safely and happily coming back. I think I am learning how much the adults around me trust me. At the same time, I am learning how to appreciate it.

The Day-1

· · · · · · ·

On the day before my flight, I suggested to my family that we spend our last night together in front of a campfire. I wanted to talk about my mental attitude towards this trip and my preparation for a long-term trip with my parents. In that case, a campfire would always be the best place to be. The campfire was a tradition that all of our family members liked, and it made everyone speechless. The firepit being in the center of us always made us feel somehow connected. It was the best suggestion I've ever made this week. My parents and I spent our last supper in front of a living fire. We did not talk about my trip much compared to my expectations. However, just sitting speechless in front of warmth under the moon in the middle of infinite darkness was enough to make the atmosphere around us calm and soft. My father seemed to have more things to say to me, but I guess he did not want to nag at me in this mood. Plus, I think he trusts me enough to not say anything. The only thing he said was, "View, sense, and think about the world beyond our world and come back safely." My mom was a different case. I could easily tell how much my mom worries about me just by looking into her eyes. She was more concerned about me than my dad was. She said numerous things, but I could also feel that she was trying to suppress herself to say fewer things than she wanted to say. It was because she knows I am kind of grown up. Also, she was aware that getting closer to the age of leaving the nest means I have to know how to handle things by myself. I was glad about my parents' trust in me. Also, I was thankful for my parents' respect for my growth. When I came back home, I checked my luggage for the last time, and I secretly put my collected paper money into an envelope. Then, I wrote a little note saying, "Thanks for sending me to Tanzania. So sorry for me demanding this much money." After my semester ended, my grade came out after a week. I felt so desperate after I checked it. I failed to get a perfect grade. To be honest and objective, it was a decent grade. However, somewhere inside me made me feel guilty. I was guilty as much as I could not tell my parents my grade. It was not because it was a terrible grade or because I did not put in my best effort. It was because I could not get the best result out of me, even though my parents decided to send me somewhere they had never been or even heard of in their lifetime. My parents have lived only in Korea, so they have some stereotypes about the place that I am going to go to tomorrow. Their stereotypes made them more concerned about their only daughter going to some mysterious place with those people. Nevertheless, they decided to send me because they trusted me. My grade not being perfect made me feel like I was betraying their trust. They showed me their best effort to trust me. Even though I knew that I put in the best effort, I doubted whether I had put in the number one effort throughout the semester or not. My resentful guilt is not the only reason I gave them money. My age was adequate to know how much this trip costs. In fact, my family is not poor. More than that, I have more privileges than other kids in the world due to our wealth. Regardless of how much my family owns, I see my parents' effort to build that wealth first. Truly speaking, our family's achievements or belongings are not due to luck. It was due to my parents' diligence over 20 or 30 years. People occasionally ask me the reason for my obsession with money. Some adults even advised me to get rid of my obsession because it does not look good. I am well aware that a 17-year-old girl being so obsessed with money makes me seem like such a girl: young and naive. Nevertheless, that cannot cover my eyes when I see my mother's hands getting wrinkled and uglier. Friends around me would never understand the feeling of looking at my father not being able to have a single meal peacefully due to his crazy ringing phone every hour and second. I am not poor. Our family is not poor. We are happily living because of my parents' effort. Looking at my parents living so hard every day makes me feel more thankful for sending me on this trip, but at the same time, it makes me an inmate fixed with a heavy chain in the colorful, splendid cell. Therefore, I decided to submit half of the allowance, which I got from my neighbors and relatives, to my parents. Compared to the trip fee, it is a piece of salt in the middle of a rice bag, but I hope that the gathered pocket money can prove my appreciation. I love you, my mom and dad. Thanks, but I am also so sorry.

D-Day

. . . .

My whole family could not sleep much. I was anxious. My mother was worried. I am not sure what made my father not sleep, but I guess he was full of thoughts and worries last night. After I woke up from only 2 hours of sleep, I could not do anything before I left home for the flight. I was just wandering around my house and waiting for my time to leave home to come. Even though it was the D-day, I was not sure whether I was really going to the continent I had only heard of. After I got tired of waiting, my dad called me out at 4 p.m. and said, "It is time to leave." My mom made sure for me to pack and bring everything for the very last time. For 3 minutes before I left my house, I made up my bed, unplugged my phone charger, and placed it in my crossbody bag. On the way to the airport, I saw a night in Seoul that I shared with my dad again. The sky seemed to be way darker than usual, but the lights of the building were shining brighter, as if they were saying goodbye to me. I could feel my mom was about to cry, but she was holding it in hard. My dad kept emphasizing to me to be truly thankful for the opportunity I got. I was not really happy to hear the repeated words, but I just agreed with my dad since it would be my last time seeing my dad before I left. When we were half way to the airport, my dad demanded that I give a kiss to my mother in the car. I like hugging and cuddling, but I honestly do not like to kiss my parents because I think I am too grown up for that. However, I just did it to be remembered as a good daughter while I was away. I am sorry, but I cannot even remember how many times I wiped out my lip. That continued even while I was on my plane. After 2 hours in the car, I finally arrived at Incheon International Airport. We were way too early. I had 1 hour left until gathering. I do not know why, but I hate airplane food, so our family decided to have a real last meal together. We went one floor down, and there was a huge food court. That day, I badly wanted to have pork cutlets, and fortunately, the food court had them. My parents did not order anything since they planned to have seafood, which Incheon is famous for, with other parents after my boarding. After I had dinner at the airport, I met my fellows and teachers. Immediately, right after I met my crew, my anxiety paused. Now, I accepted the fact that I was about to leave Korea with my schoolmates. After a long time of processing and waiting, we finally rode on a plane, but even on the way to Tanzania, I could not embrace that I was really going there. I was just being myself, without any complex thoughts along the way. I was emotionless and thoughtless. I was only a step away from being in Tanzania.

Day 1

. . . .

I cannot exactly remember how my first day went. Even after we arrived in Tanzania, we had to travel a lot more by plane since there was no direct way to Zanzibar. First, we stopped at the airport in Ethiopia. Then, we had to wait about 3 hours to get on the next plane. Even though it was tiring and boring, I was excited about how I started to feel that I was really in Africa. While I was waiting, I wandered around the airport. The airport was much cleaner, more modern, and bigger than I expected. Since I hated airplane food, I had to have lunch at the airport during our free time. Unsure what to eat and being afraid to enter the restaurant by myself, I made the simplest decision, which was Burger King. A second after I entered Burger King, I realized how much I underestimated Africa. All the options on the menu were way more expensive than I had imagined. However, I did not have a choice as I needed to eat, so I just ordered a cheeseburger for 14 US dollars. While I was waiting, one junior and three freshmen followed after me, and they also ordered their meals. After chit-chatting, my food finally came out. I guessed it took at least a little over 10 minutes to get my food. If it were in Korea, the order would not take more than 3 minutes to be completed. The time was not the part that I found ridiculous. I understood the fact that food could come out later than it did in Korea due to cultural differences. Nevertheless, I could not understand the fact that the food quality was worse than in Korea, even though I paid much more. The burger was not as pictured, and it was too small. Then, I remembered my foreign teacher from school talking about how Burger King has a uniquely finer quality in Korea. He said Burger King in other countries is terrible, and I understood what he meant right away. On the other hand, the fries were good. There was one big ketchup on the counter, and all the customers shared it. I also tried it, and it surprised me. I have visited diverse countries in my life. However, it was totally my first experience of feeling a variation of culture through ketchup. Tanzanian ketchup was more like a liquid than a solid, and it was much sweeter than the ketchup I used to taste. I was so curious as to why, so I even looked it up online, but I still couldn't even find a clue as to why it was so sweet. This was my simple and convenient first meal in Africa. After 3 hours of waiting, I finally rode on a small airplane since Zanzibar was only 2 to 3 hours away from Ethiopia. I loved how many different movies the Ethiopian airline had. I watched Mulan for a whole 2 hours. For the last 20 minutes before landing, I had trouble with my ear. My ear is as weak as a baby's, so I easily feel pain from the strong pressure of altitude. After a short period of pain, we finally arrived at our final destination, Zanzibar. Outside of the airport, I saw a few Korean children, and I was surprised to see Koreans only a minute after my arrival in Zanzibar. Also, I could not understand why they were there, but later, my biology teacher, Mr. Adams, said they were the children of missionaries. The eldest girl was Suji. The second-eldest boy was Jiho, and the third girl was Sua. Last but not least, the boy's name was Suho. I was able to recognize them as Koreans immediately because they were holding a welcome sign written in Korean. The entire missionary family welcomed us with warmth, and we rapidly rode on the bus to move to our first hotel of this vision trip. On the way to our hotel, I saw local houses, markets, buildings, apartments, and people from Zanzibar. However, the best part of everything was the cars on the road. Frankly, it is hard to say 'that' as a road. There was not a single traffic light. I never saw a single driver on the road. Cars never waited for people to pass. People just passed through in between cars. My friend, who sat next to the window, could physically feel the bus getting scratched due to friction while passing another car. We were all jolted by the fact that there was no pedestrian who was hit by the car. Our bus driver showed us a modern version of the miracle of Moses on the road, miraculously pushing through all the cars on the road. Later, our VP said, "In the USA, drivers wait until people pass. In Korea, drivers honk horns and wait for people to pass. In Tanzania, drivers honk horns and just pass." Those three sentences made us all understand the culture on the roads in this country. After we experienced the miracle, we finally arrived at our first hotel. My teacher registered my roommates. I got the same room as freshman Luna and junior Sophia.

I was comfortable with all the girls, so I did not have any complaints and liked my roommates. We all went up to the third floor and faced the room for the first time. It turned out to be better than I thought. Our room was wide in size and had three beds, and one of them was a twin bed. The only problem that my roommates and I were worried about was bugs. All the windows were not completely closed. There were all cracks in between, so there was no doubt that we would face tons of bugs in one day of staying here. Later, we filled our room with smoke from bug spray. We went down for dinner. The pastor from our school officially introduced the missionary's family to Lobby, and the missionary gave us a few warnings. She told us not to drink water from the sink or any other place except from bottles. She told us not to eat any seafood from the local market and not to drink any fruit juice from the local market. After brief warnings, we went to the most famous night market in Zanzibar. We sat at the main table of a small street restaurant. Tanzanian teens were dumping themselves into the water right next to us. As I recall my memory again, I wish I would have jumped into the ocean while the teachers were out of sight. The waiter came to our table and sang "Jambo Bwana" for us. I loved how everyone was so energetic. After we waited a few minutes, our dinner was served. We tried chicken, skewered food, and Zanzibar pizza. All the street food was, fortunately, way more tasty than I expected. Even before I left Korea, I had worried about food the most. I was relieved after finally experiencing it. Additionally, we drank Passion Fanta, which was only available in Tanzania. It was sweet, but the aftertaste was sour and a little bit bitter. Also, it was extremely addictive. All the students loved it. After dinner, it was getting too late, so we came back to our hotel right away. Today ended like this. We will start our wall painting tomorrow, so I better go to sleep early. Bye, first night of Zanzibar.

Day 2

. . . .

My day began at 6 a.m. I did not have to wake up that early, but I guess I did not get used to the jet lag yet. Instead of messing around on the bed, I decided to have a cup of cold water and do a morning workout, since I did not want to waste my first morning in Zanzibar. After my brief 35 minutes of working out, I took a quick shower and went down for breakfast. I did not have huge expectations for this hotel breakfast, but I actually liked it. Four types of tropical fruit, traditional Tanzanian loaves of bread, baked potatoes, fried eggs, three types of juice, and other common bread with several jams were served. The watermelon was much worse than I expected, but the mango was fine. Since my stomach usually gets sensitive in the morning, I decided to simply have a light breakfast of toast with jam and small pieces of fruit instead of challenging my stomach. After our first breakfast in Zanzibar, we got our phones back. Yesterday, our teacher decided to take our phones away before dismissing us to sleep. It was for putting us to sleep and making us closer to nature than phone screens. Zanzibar is 6 hours ahead of Seoul, so the time right after breakfast was the perfect time to contact my parents. My mother sounded worried about me the entire day. She said she slept in my bedroom last night. It was clear that she would do that for the rest of the vision trip. After my brief report to parents, we got on the bus to go to Hope School. Hope School is a missionary's school located in an exclusive area of Zanzibar. The area that the school was in was not for tourists, so the distance gap was vast, which made us stay in the bus for at least an hour. The distance itself was the main problem, but the chaotic road was another reason for us to get on the bus right after 30 minutes of breakfast. For today, we were not supposed to meet any students yet. We started our wall painting today, which made the art department students genuinely busy last night and even when we were in Korea. Before we came to Tanzania, we were broken down into 4 departments for education and volunteer work: art, PE, English, and music. I was not in charge of art since I was in the English department. However, regardless of which departments students were in, all students were supposed to do wall painting today since it was undoubtedly going to be a lot of work. When we finally arrived at Hope School, the raindrops were heavily falling. While we were under the school ceiling and listening to rain, the VP told us that Zanzibar is not meant to be rainy this much. That heavy rain was due to environmental pollution. It was an experience of the real result of not recycling, using too much detergent and shampoo, and wasting water and food. When I got environmental education a few years ago at my school, I learned that daily habits of overusing can impact the earth. Nonetheless, I could not embrace what I learned wholeheartedly at that time. Now, I truly believe what I was taught. Heavy rain did not only result in my enlightenment, but it also led to delays. We had to wait until the rain stopped. For the art students, they did not have time to rest because of sketching. For the rest of us, we were so bored and hoped for the rain to stop. While we were waiting, we met some local students. Today was not their school day, but they just visited school for fun. About 7 to 10 years old, five children looked at us merrily. They seemed not to speak English, which made me concerned about classes that will happen next week. We have to run classes in English, but if they cannot understand

English, that will absolutely challenge us. After a long wait, we could finally start our wall painting. The process was not as complicated as it may seem. What we had to do was fill out the particular part of the wall that Art Department students had already sketched. I did not choose the art department because my major was not art. Nevertheless, drawing on the wall has always been on my bucket list. I was allotted the color seaweed. It was enjoyable at first. Later, I realized how tiring and tedious the work is. Coloring while not crossing the sketched line on the wall was not as easy as I presumed. My wrist hurt, and I was sweating so bad. When I was coloring the wall, I felt like I was coloring the vacant house in a local area in Korea for volunteer work, not at Hope School located in Zanzibar. I was still questioning whether I was certainly in Africa or not. However, whenever I looked outside, children were running and giggling among themselves, which reminded me that I was really in Zanzibar. After the wall painting, we had our lunch at Hope School with local teachers. We encountered local food for the first time. Honestly, I was afraid to try it, and my fear was right. The local food was not for me. The leaf vegetable and bean curry were served, and it was too slimy, and I am not sure which word to use to describe the taste. So, I just had rice and a Korean side dish prepared for us. Thankfully, the missionary family prepared a Korean side dish because they expected that we might be reluctant to eat the local food. Even though we had the Korean side dish, lots of students did not finish their dishes. I looked at a pile of leftover food from us, and I turned my eyes to a pile of empty plates from the local teachers. I realized how wrong we were, and my school's pastor pointed out our leftover food. From tomorrow on, I decided not to leave any leftovers. After a short period of lunch, we began our second stage of wall painting. Everyone worked so hard. Honestly, I did not expect them to work this hard, and I have to admit that I underestimated them. After working, it was time to wash our brushes. I went to the sink next to the school, and we washed the brushes with our bare hands so passionately. The paint inside the brush was stuck in between, and it never fell apart. While we were washing the brushes, one of the local women came next to us, and she started glaring at us. I even smiled and said "Hi" to her, but she still looked so mad at us, and I could not understand her. Later, the missionary came and had a conversation with her. Then, I understood what was wrong. The old bucket that one of our students was using for washing brushes belonged to her. The missionary said, "She uses that bucket for washing laundry, cooking, and washing kids." I felt like something smashed into my head. We easily assumed the bucket would be trashed because it looked so old and unavailable. We never expected that the bucket could be used for cooking. I was not the one who used it, but I strongly felt sorry for her. The missionary promised to buy her another new bucket. I quietly said, "Sorry," to her. She seemed not to accept my apology. There was another fact that made my brain freeze. The missionary said the sink we were messing with paint was the only place that was available with clean water in this whole town. That fact hit my head. I was aware that about two hundred people live in this town, but I could never assume this was the only place for water. More than that, we were messing with that precious spot with stuck paint. I felt so guilty, and I am sure everyone was as guilty as I was. We cleaned the sink as much as we could, but acrylic paint was not meant to wash out. I wanted to clean the place more, but it was time to leave the school. I explained my apology to the missionary, and she said she would ask the school's employees to clean the sink. On the bus, I pondered whether we were really helpful today. I hope we were, but it is certain that we have to be more helpful than today. I made up my mind to be more productive tomorrow. After we arrived at the hotel, we were given one hour of shower time. We were all covered in paint, so we definitely had to wash it out. One hour can sound pretty enough, but when three people have to shower in one hour, it is actually very insufficient. We quickly took a shower and gathered. If someone asked me which product to use to erase acrylic paint stains on the body, I would answer that question with "toner." The toner erased all the paint stains on my body. I even loaned it to one of my teachers, Henry and Eric. I wanted to lend it to other friends, too, but I had to save it for the rest of the 13 days. For Mr.Adams, I lent it to him since he was my favorite teacher. For Eric, he took on the privilege of being my boyfriend. For Henry, I had to lend him since I painted his back when we were coloring the wall. After gathering at the lobby, we went to a restaurant near the hotel. We arrived at a Western food restaurant, and the food itself was fine. However, I still do not understand why it took more than an hour to get all our food. The servers were really slow and tended to forget things easily. I had to repeat my sentences several times to get a cup. My impatient personality really did not like this part of Tanzania. Also, while we were waiting, we realized another factor that delayed our food. The restaurant did not have enough plates, so whenever we finished our dishes, the servers had to take them back right away to put other menus on those plates and serve them. I was shocked and tired of waiting, but I admitted that I had to get used to this cultural difference. As a result, it took 2 hours to finish all the dishes. After our dinner, our teachers brought us to a famous gelato store right in front of the restaurant. I chose the lime taste, and it was too sour for me. I tried my friends' gelato, and theirs was tasty. After the dessert, we came back to the hotel, and the teachers made us gather at the lobby again. The VP said we will play a bingo game, which will last the whole Tanzania trip. We were ordered to fill out the bingo with the goals we wanted to accomplish until the end of the trip. I thought that was a really good idea because we can improve ourselves by accomplishing those goals. My goals were like 'Be more intimate with teachers and VP,' 'Hug at least one local person,' and 'Learn the local language, Swahili.' After filling out our bingo, our electronic devices were taken away. Today ends, and we will go snorkeling tomorrow. I am really looking forward to it. Bye, second night of Zanzibar.

Day 3

. . . .

Today, we did not wake up super early like yesterday. When we came down for breakfast, we were all wearing our swimming outfits because today was snorkeling day. This was the part where I got most excited for this vision trip. Snorkeling is one of my favorite activities because I love swimming and water at the same time. I did not have a heavy breakfast since I did not want to be seasick. Instead of digging for breakfast, I was busy wearing a thick sunscreen swimsuit. I was aware of how strong America's sunlight is because I had experienced it. I also knew Africa's sunlight was even stronger. I badly wanted to protect my skin. I did not stop putting on my sunscreen, even though my roommates freaked out. After a short preparation, we finally gathered and got on the bus. It took about an hour to get to the ocean. Even after we arrived at the ocean, our journey continued. We had to ride on a wooden boat to get to the island and the middle of the Indian Ocean. We rode on the small wooden boat with our flippers. Then, we had to transfer to a bigger wooden boat in the middle of the ocean. It was not easy to move the boat since we had to balance weight to not make the boat flip. The captains of the main boat welcomed us and served us cool sodas with pineapples. We had to reach a small island for swimming and pictures before our snorkeling started. I have visited numerous oceans in my life, but this was my first time in the Indian Ocean. Before I came to Tanzania, I looked up Tanzania on social media, and everyone was complimenting the emerald ocean. What they were saying was absolutely right. The ocean was exquisite. The transparent greenish-emerald ocean welcomed us. It was so transparent that I could vividly see pinkish-white corals inside the water, which aroused my excitement for snorkeling more. Another part I loved was the boat itself. It was like a boat from a children's movie. It has always been my dream to ride on the boat from the movie. When I was lying on the rope of the boat, I felt like I popped out of the movie. I put my head inside the water and cut the emerald ocean. It was my first time feeling closer to nature in Tanzania. After enjoying my movie moments and taking thousands of pictures on the boat, we finally arrived at the small island. It was really small. It was the size of my living room plus the kitchen. The captain said we would stay here for 30 minutes, swimming and taking photos. The island was the best spot for pictures, but we did not have time for that. We immediately threw ourselves into the water and felt the refreshing water. I worried about my sunscreen melting, but water splashing from my friends made me totally forget about my skin. While we were messing around splashing water on each other like we were 7-year-old kids in the swimming pool, Mr. Adams jumped into the water and dipped us into the water. I do not exactly remember how the other three teachers played, but I can vividly recall my memory of Mr. Adams playing. My stereotypes of teachers totally broke down into pieces. He splashed water on us, and he seemed to enjoy it a lot. It was my first time encountering a different side of the teacher that made me realize that I felt too distant from all of my teachers. At that time, I felt confident that I would face all the humane and real characteristics of the teachers during this vision trip. I would feel closer and more intimate with all of them as a student and as a person. Just like Mr. Adams did, we poured him water and dipped each other. After the entertaining 30 minutes ended, we rode on the boat again to go snorkeling. We moved to the middle of the ocean again and stopped at the snorkeling spot. Our captain explained the rules and put toothpaste on our goggles for us to see the ocean clearly. Since it was my second or third time doing snorkeling, I rejected the life jacket and dove into the water. I was puzzled by the strong waves at first. However, I found my balance and put my face in the water. Then, I saw a scene from the movie Mermaid. Colorful groups of fish were swimming between colorful corals. I was so amazed by the fact that this kind of beautiful scene can exist in real life and that it was just hiding underwater. I wanted to catch one of the fish, but whenever I tried to get closer, it ran away from me. When I put my face up, I saw my other friends dipping their faces into the water. Half of them wore life jackets, and half of them did not. My other female friends, Olivia and Mia, were too frightened to give it a try. So, I went up to the boat. After a short inhale, I explained to Mia why she must do it and demonstrated the scene I just saw underwater. It looked like it was Olivia's first attempt at snorkeling, so she was practicing breathing in goggles with Mr. Adams. Mia was finally persuaded by many people around her, wore a life jacket, and dove into the water. For my second dive, I also put on a life jacket because my body got exhausted so easily from strong waves. I needed something for me to depend on. Mia did not fear the water that much. When I turned my eyes from Mia, I saw Ms. Ruby floating far away from our boat. I swam directly to her and pulled her closer to our boat. However, I had to repeat that a few more times because she floated a few more times. It was so hilarious to find out that my teacher is actually not good at swimming. Also, it was humorous to rescue my teacher and feel protective instincts toward her. I felt like something was the opposite. When I turned my eyes again, I found Olivia drowning in the water. Again, I swam towards her. Then, an unexpected situation happened. Olivia grabbed me hard out of her fear. I was so surprised and dazed. Then, I lost my balance in the water. I started to flounder with her. I told her several times to stop grasping my arms and shoulders, but it was pointless. She could not hear because my mouth was spitting out water while I was yelling in the water. The life jacket saved me. I finally balanced it with the support of the life jacket and told her not to grab me. I pulled her and placed her hand on the side of the boat, and she was pulled up by the captain and Mr. Adams. Then she seemed to finally find relief. After a short, chaotic event, I was enjoying myself. Then, the captain told everyone to come up. I was confused. I did not want to leave the water, but he told us the dolphins appeared near this area, so we had to move right now. Everyone quickly got up, and the captain turned the boat in a rush. I prayed hard to see the dolphins. Due to our sincere prayers, our pastor saw the fin of the dolphin. I could not see the fin. However, the whole group of dolphins finally appeared. There were about 4 to 5. I had seen dolphins several times in my life, but it was my first time seeing dolphins this close without a glass wall. Everyone got so excited when they saw dolphins. We were standing in front of others and unintentionally blocking each other's sights. Also, I admit that one of them was me. We took thousands of pictures and turned our boat into another snorkeling section. That area was so shallow that I could stand up on the sand. The caption said we can meet fish closely here, but I saw none due to the fluttering sand in the water. However, I was not disappointed because the area itself was gorgeous with nature. I liked how the water got blueish when we got here because it goes along with the greenish plants on the rocks around us pretty well. I decided that place was not for snorkeling, and we got on the boat again to have lunch. For lunch, we went to another island, and we had a seafood buffet. There were not many kinds of menus, but lobsters and shrimp were delectable. Everyone loved the lunch, especially me; I had more than two plates. I also loved the fruit dessert, which was composed of watermelon, passion fruit, grapefruit, etc. After lunch, we had to go back to our original land. We rode on the boat with tired bodies and heavy eyes. On the way back to the land, we sang a few songs together, and the captains actually loved us singing. Also, I was able to make unforgettable memories. Whenever I flashback my memory on the boat, the scene of our pastor singing alone on the boat with a wide, beautiful blue sky as background pops up in my head. When we finally arrived after a short concert, the captains appreciated our respect and manners towards them. I felt overwhelmed by their gratitude. I assume it was my first time being appreciated by being respectful. I wondered whether there were a lot of people who were mean to them or not. I didn't mean it, but I feel so thankful for their gratitude at the same time. I will never forget our four captains. They waved their hands until I could not see them. At night, after the simple dinner, we got our free time earlier than usual. We had a lot of free time because our dance practice ended earlier than I expected. When we were preparing our education in Korea, we also decided to give out some performances for local people to enjoy. I was allotted to the dance department since I had experienced dancing on the stage several times. Our practice even continued after our arrival in Tanzania. I was so exhausted from dancing after a long day of swimming, but dancing with my school people on the roof of the hotel under the night sky with stars was breathtaking. Due to my bad eyesight, I could not see the sky clearly, but the shine from the stars proved to me that they were illuminating somewhere up there. Dance made me totally sweat. I wanted to calm myself down immediately. Then, I was sure it was time to accomplish my other bucket list, which was swimming at night. I loved swimming, but safety always held me back from swimming at night. After I got certain that this would be almost the only day we could swim at night because we had not started our education service yet, I started to gather people. I assembled about eight people. Some of them didn't want to join us, but I guess we looked so fun, so they joined us in the middle. The 10th graders, Ian and Arthur, brought their guitars. I put their legs in the water and began singing and playing guitar. Next to them, our second round of water was announced, and we messed around. Then, I looked up at the sky. The sky was full of stars. There were more stars than there were when we were dancing. The night at Zanzibar reminded me of the night in Seoul I shared with my dad. My curiosity about Zanzibar's night was solved. It was more beautiful than I imagined. I learned that even though we look up at the same sky, it can look much different. I will never forget the fellows I shared my night with. Bye, third night of Zanzibar.

Day 4

. . . .

Sunday morning came. Our school is a Christian school, which means they hope we attend church on Sunday. However, there isn't a church for us in Zanzibar, so we decided to go to a missionary's house for worship. The VP and pastor emphasized that we should wear socks and proper shoes for today. Since the missionary family was inviting us to their own home, we had to show some respect. I couldn't wake up early today because I slept super late last night as we went swimming. I would swim all night if one of the teachers did not stop us. They did not say anything until 2 a.m. because they liked that we were making memories and getting closer to each other. However, our noises kept them away from sleep, so one of the teachers finally dismissed us. I felt sorry for keeping them awake, but that could not keep me from starving. I unpacked my first ramen in Zanzibar at 2 a.m. and had ramen with my roommate, Sophia. Luna had already gone to bed due to heavy swimming that day. The ramen made my face severely swollen and my stomach feel greasy. Nevertheless, I never regretted my experience or decision to eat ramen last night. After quickly dressing up, I went down and apologized for waking the teachers. Fortunately, they seemed to understand, since they wanted us to build up our memories. After a brief breakfast (the same one as we got yesterday), we got on the bus. The missionary's house was so far away, as it was deep in the forest. The phone service was unavailable, and the road was wild. When we finally arrived, the missionary's house was the only big and fine house among the other houses. The missionaries and their children welcomed us with their hearts. Right after we got in, we sat in a circle and prepared for worship. Before we left the hotel, we had scores of worship songs to sing during worship. Our school's pastor took out his guitar and started the worship. He said, "Missionaries in front of you shared a lot of love with people here for 15 years. However, it seemed like they could not get enough love compared to the love they shared. We are here today to refill the love they shared with others. Let's sing for them." Then, we gathered our two hands and put our hands towards them politely while singing. Even though I was not Christian, I felt some connections with people there. I felt choked up and overwhelmed inside my heart. When I turned my eyes to one of the missionaries' faces, I saw him sobbing and wiping his face. After praise, a male missionary stood up and started his preaching. To be honest, I am not Christian, so I have zero interest in sermons. However, the thing that got my attention was not the Christian's words, but the story of the missionaries. He said he met his wife here 15 years ago, married her, and had three children. He and his wife dedicated their lives to helping children here and teaching them to live better lives. Later, my VP said that most missionaries are reluctant to come to countries like Tanzania since it is such hard work. Most missionaries want to go to countries like the USA or countries located in Europe. Both missionaries came here with their wills. I imagined myself dedicating my life here to helping others. I pondered deeply, and I reached the conclusion that I could not do it. I cannot put my whole life here to give children better lives. After my conclusion, I started to respect them. I guess my other crews began to respect them, too. After worship, the female missionary prepared lunch for us. I missed Korean food so much, so it was the best news I heard so far. The lunch was Korean fried squid and Korean chicken stew. I felt like I was in Korea. We all enjoyed it very much. After lunch, we said goodbye and left the missionary's house, which means we had free time for the whole afternoon. For the afternoon, I decided to try dreadlocks at a local shop. My friends and I went to the local market to find a hairdresser. We found one of the shops with hairdressers and did our hair. While I was waiting for my turn, I looked around the shops and talked to local people there. I met Peace and Wanda. I cannot remember others' names since their names were too long for me to remember. I was almost the last one to have my hair braided. It took about a little bit more than 20 minutes to do my hair. I loved my braided hair, but it was more satisfying to look at my friends' hair. They looked so different than usual. Due to a longer hairdressing time than we had expected, we joined the rest of our crew a little bit late. When we came across other members who had not had their hair braided, they all burst into laughter as soon as our eyes met. One of my friends said I look like an alien from a webtoon. After we had dinner outside, we came back to the hotel and encountered a tremendous scene inside. Swarms of unknown, tiny bugs were attached to each wall. All of the students wanted to go to their rooms immediately, but we could not because we had to do our last preparation for tomorrow's education. We stood uncomfortably in the lobby, and whenever I saw a dot on my laptop's screen, it was a tiny bug that fell from the roof. Later, I got used to it and threw it away. Plus, I got why there were so many bugs inside the hotel. It was because the hotel never closed the main door, and the four sides of the roof were not completely covered, but they were covered with curtains. Despite this situation, we still had to have our meeting. I don't even remember what we talked about. The only thing I can remember is that all the people from the English department braided their hair, so we promised to keep this hair as long as we could to show it to local students when we start our education tomorrow. After our meeting, students who were staying on the third floor gathered all together, including me and my roommates, because there were too many bugs in our rooms. Just like I worried on the first day, the cracks between windows were the best passageways for tiny bugs to enter our hotel room. For our room, at least the windows were closed. In the room next to us, the windows were wide open due to the hotel cleaning lady. I still do not get why, but the hotel people always open our windows after cleaning. (Maybe for fresh air?) After I realized that fact, I asked the receptionist to not open the windows after cleaning, so our room was better than others. We were standing desperately and waiting for people to come to help us. We were all thinking about the same thing: 'This is the toughest day until now.' When the cleaning person came, he swept the floor of our room, and a pile of bugs appeared on his dustpan. Honestly, it freaked me out. We were all feeling the same thing. Then, I suddenly felt sorry because I felt like I was being rude to him. I felt like I was overreacting when this should be one of their normal days. If I were the cleaner, I would feel offended if some foreigners freaked out when they faced one of my normal days and made the queasy faces we just made. I apologized for overreacting and thanked him for cleaning our rooms. Then we all went into rooms. It was still full of dead and alive bugs, but we were too exhausted to bother it, so we decided to live with it. We even named the bugs to make them feel intimate. We called them Sebastian. Tomorrow is going to be my first teaching day. All of the English department students are not confident. I hope we can do better than we imagined right now. Bye, fourth night of Zanzibar.

Day 5

. . . .

We woke up at 6 a.m. because today we had to explain why we came here. I packed all my needs and got on the bus. The sky was covered in gray clouds, and it was about to rain. All our nerves and worries were gone when the day finally came. We sang songs and chit-chatted on the way to school. After our arrival, we carried out all the materials, and we were allocated to each classroom. The classroom did not have a door, and the big dog was yawning next to our classroom. We decided to name the dog Chunsam. Our class started right away. Since children were in the age range of two to elementary school second grade, our class time was only 30 minutes due to their lack of concentration. I underestimated 30 minutes; I did not know 30 minutes was this long. I realized how hard it is to lead the class and the students' concentration. Sophia and I shouted out an alphabet song. As I said before, their English was not sufficient to listen to class in English. Therefore, a local teacher joined each class and translated our words into Swahili, but the main problem was the students' lack of participation. I understand them because I would be frightened, too, if a teacher from a country far away came into my class and demanded that I shout A. They were too shy and a little bit stunned, so we smiled as much as we could and showed them the best reaction we could when they participated. After the 30 minutes that felt like 30 years finally ended, all of my friends came out of the classrooms, and they looked like their souls were sucked by dementors. Everyone complained about the students' lack of participation. After a 5-minute break that felt like 5 seconds had ended, we started our second class; this class was better. Like every class in the world, there is always one student who eases the teacher's burden. The second class had two of those students. It was much easier to handle this class. They were 6 to 7 years old. I cannot differentiate between students yet. Now, I understand why white people say it is so hard to differentiate Asians. After the second period, it was snack time. Students and I had local pastries, and they tasted like twisted doughnuts from Korea. When we were chewing our pastries, the rain suddenly started to fall heavily. Rain resulted in delays again because students could not cross the playground between classrooms. For our extra break time, I played with the toddlers. Now I realize how adorable and cute they were. I am not usually a child person, but I loved all the reactions they showed us whenever we tickled them. I do not know her name, but I love the girl in the dark green dress with a runny nose and big monolid eyes. She definitely had an ideal, pretty face. I like her because her smile is innocent. Another girl who liked me was really slim and wearing a fancy red dress. She liked me because she was the first girl I was extra nice to. I just wanted some students to remember me well, so I was being extra nice sometimes. After the rain stopped, we had two more classes, and we were out of energy. We were free after the morning classes since it was summer camp, not daily classes. All my fellows gathered in the main hall of the school, and we were all out of energy. Then, our lunch arrived. It was rice, a local side dish, and kimchi that the missionary prepared at dawn for us. The only things I could eat were kimchi and rice. I tried the local food, but, as usual, it wasn't for me. However, as I promised myself on the first day I came to Hope School, I did not make any leftovers. None of my friends made leftovers, either. I finished my lunch earlier than others, so I was sitting outside. That's where I saw children across the street. They seemed interested in me. I got closer to them and said hi. With my photographer teacher, two of us went on a tour of a local town under the permission of the missionaries. It is actually not okay to enter the local people's towns by ourselves because we can be in danger. It was a really rare chance to visit local people's houses safely. I met a lot of children. They all seemed interested in me. Whenever I took out my phone, they ran to me and demanded that I take pictures of them. I still don't know why they loved taking pictures that much because they could never get those pictures from me. Perhaps they love posing. Around the children, there were few adults, and there were few adults saying "Carribu" to me. It meant "welcome." I responded with "Asante," which means "Thank you." One of the women kindly introduced me to the whole town. She showed me inside her house. I left my face with a smile to hide my feelings that could make her uncomfortable. I was shocked at how dirty and small the house is. There were no windows. Obviously, there was only one bed, which was intended for at least 6 to 8 people to sleep in. They depended on one single battery as the source to brighten up their houses. The kitchen was made of three firewoods. There was no real restroom or bathroom. I was shocked and unintentionally felt kind of uncomfortable, but I did not want my feelings to be expressed on my face or body because I would feel bad if someone showed me a disgusted face after seeing my room. She also showed me many natural features of the town. She held a cat and asked me to take a picture of her. She introduced me to her goat. She took me to a coconut tree and explained it to me. It was interesting to see coconut trees growing inside the town. On my way to the tour, the children always pursued me and held my hands. I was glad to have them with me because they were all such good kids. Plus, they listened to me well.

I am not a child person, but I had no problem being with them since they all had good attitudes towards me. After a short time, I joined my crew again. Then, our afternoon work started. We were asked to do physical work this time. We had to move heavy earth materials to the other side of the school by using hands, shovels, and a cart. I was not assigned to the shovels because I was a girl, but I hated that. None of them knew, but I had countless experiences using shovels during my childhood. I was unique because I loved physical labor, and my grandfather was open to teaching me. After a few minutes, I looked at boys using shovels, which was totally disappointing. It was so clear that they had no experience using a tool like that. I grabbed one of the shovels and showed them how to use it. Then, without even me knowing it, I was in charge of the shovel. I was happy to do it, and teachers were impressed by me. However, there was one problem that I could not think of. Although I am much better with shovels, my innate physical strength is different from that of males. It was hard to follow their speed, but I did not want to whine. Therefore, I did my best among the 3 boys and 1 male teacher next to me. Even the local teacher was worried about me. My passion resulted in my muscle pain in the bus on the way back to our hotel. At 4 p.m., the schedule for today was finished, and we all went back to the hotel. I had to unbraid my hair due to sweat. After the shower and dinner, I felt a strong stomach ache. I guessed I got an upset stomach after the sudden active muscle movements and greasy food. I thought I could bear it, but later I burst into tears a bit when I was massaged to relax my muscles. Fortunately, I felt okay right after the massage, and I was warned by many members of my group to not work too hard. I was not happy to be the first one to be sick in the group, and I was not glad with the result of working hard. I hope I can feel better tomorrow. Bye, fifth night of Zanzibar.

Day 6

. . . .

Just like yesterday, we had a busy morning and went to school. For today, I was the leading teacher of the English class instead of the sub-teacher. I felt like I could do much better than yesterday. Today, our first class was the youngest grade of this school, which is made up of children between ages 2 and 3. They were too small to remain seated. I cannot recall my memory well because it was too out of control. One of the kids ran out of the class. One of the kids slept. None of them sang the alphabet song. Later in the class, I put one of the students on my lap to make her concentrate. The class time just vanished, and I am not sure whether I did fine or not. Later, I figured out that the average time that a 2- to 3-year-old can focus is 7 to 9 minutes. Then, I could understand how hard that 30-minute class was for them. After the most chaotic first period, the rest of the class students looked like angels to me. They were much more relaxed than they were yesterday. A lot of them sang the alphabet song with me. It was much better to lead those three classes. In the afternoon, after the kids left, I felt my throat hurt from screaming too much. During lunch time, my friends and I sat perched on the edge of the stairs outside and messed around with a dog that we named Chunsam. We also found another dog, and we named her Chunsik. The missionary said she is carrying babies and will deliver them soon. We all wished to see babies before we left Tanzania. For today, Mr. Adams allotted me to put up the maps in school instead of hard labor under the sunlight. He was worrying about my condition. Later, Sophia told me she actually asked him to take me out of the physical labor because she was also worried about me. Mr. Adams agreed with her because he cared about me, too. I felt thankful for both of them. After the afternoon work was done, we all went back to the hotel, took a shower, and went to have dinner. We had chicken for dinner, and the plating was so pretty. All of us took pictures of the food. I did not eat much because I was afraid of getting a stomach ache again due to greasy food. When we were halfway done with our food, we could hear Salsa songs, which grabbed our interest. The man was about to give a salsa dance lesson, and 90 percent of the students joined the class. We all followed men's movements, and when it was time for boys to hold girls' hands, They were really shy. It was really fun to watch my male friends try to be gentlemen. For me, I did not feel any awkwardness since I was just holding my boyfriend's hands. It was my first time holding my boyfriend's hands in Tanzania. We could not be together easily due to the eyes of teachers who worried about one couple in the group messing around the whole group's atmosphere, which we never planned to do. I and Eric had no choice, so we kind of forced ourselves to be away from each other, which gave me a lot of stress and made me realize how hard it is to be in a group. Eric gently held my hands and led me. Other boys led the girls, and girls followed the lead of the boys. It was such a fun, quality time. Our teachers, who did not want to interfere with our quality time, could not stop us and let us dance for 2 hours. The salsa delayed our schedule, but everyone loved it, and I could never forget about it. Bye, sixth night of Zanzibar.

Day 7

. . . .

Just like usual, we all woke up super early and rode on the bus. Instead of teaching, today I was in charge of painting. All of the students from every department took their turns and used one of the teaching days to work on the wall paintings because the teachers wanted us to obtain various experiences. I preferred to be in class because the sunlight was too strong. I painted the restroom alone, and I kind of felt apart because of the gap between being alone and being surrounded by many students. I got irritated because I was not good at painting and the weather was too hot all of a sudden. While I was painting the wall aggressively in a bad mood, the cool, fresh air went through my body. It calmed my body temperature from head to toe. I suddenly felt relaxed and relieved. I realized the importance and value of this cool, fresh air. I also realized how I could easily feel terrible. I noticed how everyone here has to live in this hot weather in much worse conditions than the conditions I am living in here now. I felt embarrassed. For the first time in my life, I felt thankful for the air. I realized how everyone here could be thankful for small things. On the other side of my heart, I felt sad for myself because I would not be able to appreciate things as much as people here do in life. After all the classes were finished, I joined my department again, and we had our lunch. The quality of the Korean side dish the missionary prepared for us was getting better and better. I also realized the rice was becoming Asian-style. I realized that the missionaries asked a cook for a favor at the school. My friends and I felt strongly thankful for them. After lunch, we spent the whole afternoon painting. It was tiring, but I was glad that we could finish most of the wall painting today. Tomorrow is going to be the last day of teaching. Tonight, all English department students gathered and prepared games and gifts for students. Plus, we could not sleep until 11 p.m. because we had to practice the performances we prepared in Korea. The day after tomorrow is sports day, and our school has prepared performances for it. I was in the dance department, so we danced under the moonlight until 11 p.m. today. Mr. Adams, who was the head of the dance department, worried about whether we could do well on the stage, so we practiced so hard together until 11 p.m., either. I was out of energy physically and mentally, but I was worried about our dance team, too. I hope we can end our teaching pretty well tomorrow and have sports day on Friday. Bye, seventh night of Zanzibar.

Day 8

. . . .

Today is the last day of teaching. Yesterday night, our English Department students could not sleep until 1 a.m. because we were busy with the preparation of games for today. We prepared a treasure hunt for children, and Simon says As a prize, we prepared a lot of alphabet jelly for them. For the first time in four days, we did not have class inside the classroom. We all planned to bring children to the school hall. I felt sorry for the children for 4 days because we were all well aware that our class was the most boring out of all the other classes. In the other classes, children danced, sang, colored, or did experiments, but for our class, all they had to do was remain seated and listen. That's why we prepared a lot of physical activities for the last class. Before we brought the children to the school hall, we already hid the alphabet papers all around the hall, so the children could find them and we could treat them with jellies. For the first class, I was in charge of leading the class. I led the children to the hall and started the class by explaining the rules of the game. It was quite easy for us, but I explained it in detail as much as I could since it was their first time encountering this kind of game. It was simple. In the game, they must find the hidden alphabet that I command, and I give them alphabet jelly as a reward. I worried that they might not understand it well, but it turned out they loved it. They were so enthusiastic to find papers and get jellies. Plus, it helped them a lot to learn and memorize the alphabet. All four classes loved this game. I thought we should have done this earlier. For the last 5 minutes of class, we all sang alphabet songs. Students were sitting around me, and I was in the middle of them. I felt like I was Maria from The Sound of Music. After all the classes, the 9th graders gathered to give them the goody bags we prepared for them. The missionary explained that the gifts were prepared by us, and we started to hand them our small goody bags. It took a few days to pack and sort out the goody bags. Honestly, I kind of regretted my decision in the middle of preparation because there were so many things to pack. However, I was so glad to see their happy faces, and I never regretted doing that. Before students were dismissed, they shouted out some Swahili so enthusiastically while hitting their chests. The Swahili means "I am so important. I am born to be loved." The missionary said they yell out those phrases every day before they go home. I got all choked up after hearing this. I was sure that I was at the right place to help. This school was not just teaching knowledge;

it was also teaching them values. After all the tiring schedule (as usual), we got on the bus and heard the news that we would get a longer break today. We were all so happy because the break/shower time was insufficient for three girls to take a shower. We went back to our hotel and were so exhausted. However, this country never lets us take a break. Hear me out. Something happened that I can't even imagine would occur in Korea: some of our rooms got overbooked. First of all, I could not understand why the room got overbooked. Second, I believe it can happen, but I blamed the sky for happening to me. Third, I really did not understand why the hotel urged us to move our rooms since we booked the rooms first. This story actually started on the first day we arrived at this hotel. We already got told that we might have to move our rooms because they got overbooked. Later, I found out how common this situation is here. However, they changed their words because our teachers politely asked them to somehow help us stay as one. For sure, they said we could stay here. No packing. No moving. No hauling the suitcase. Nevertheless, a few days later, the hotel assured us that we would move our rooms after a few days. Well, that's where we started our war. We explained what they said, but we figured out the communication among themselves is really, um, not good. What manager 1 knew and what manager 2 knew were different, and they each believed that they were right. Later, the hotel agreed to their miscommunication and apologized to us. However, the fact that some of us had to move into the rooms did not change. We talked to the missionary, too, but she said the argument will not change anything here. Therefore, we just accepted our fates and decided to think of this as just an unfortunate situation that can happen to foreigners. My room, Henry's room, and Mr. Adams room got chosen by fate. All of us packed everything and put the suitcase out this morning. I wasn't that mad until this point. I wasn't. This is where I got pissed off. After we came back to the hotel, they started to say some nonsense, suddenly saying that we could stay in our rooms, but the room was already given to others. They said we could stay in the room next to ours, but it was already occupied by one of our students. Our teachers had to argue with them for an hour. I saw alive dissonance at that time. Some of them were trying to transport our suitcases. Some of them waited. Some of them argued with our teachers. At the end, there is no change to the fact that we are moving, so we all started to haul the suitcases. The reason why we so badly did not want to move our rooms is that those rooms are not in the building we used to stay in. We had to pass through some allies to get to another building. Well, what made me feel a little better was that our rooms got a little bit better. Plus, they were still very kind and nice to me, so I quit staying mad. After we unpacked everything again, we went to the building where we used to stay and started the meeting for the last day at Hope School. Tomorrow is sports day. It will really be the last day of visiting homeschool. Also, tomorrow is D-day for all performances. I hope we do not make any big mistakes, at least. Bye, eighth night of Tanzania.

Day 9

· · · · · · ·

Today is D-day for performances and sports. On the way to school, we were singing, listening to the songs, and dancing to not make any mistakes on the stage. I crossed my fingers for all of us. When we arrived at Hope School, we did not have any specific duty to do. Our main duty was to stick with village dwellers and help them with games. We were sitting backstage with students. The games began, and we were just watching the villagers play games. Rather than focusing on the games, we were more interested in messing around with students backstage. I taught them

Salsa routines and the Korean clapping game. Some of them were really getting it. Then, I turned my eyes and spotted Yummna looking at a video of the ocean flow from one of our phones. She looked so amazed and focused. Her big eyes were admiring and glaring. Then, I realized it would be her first time watching the ocean. I was curious about what she would be feeling right now. My friends also participated in some games with the dwellers. It was obviously a tedious and worn-out game for us. However, we tried our best to show an enjoyable attitude towards them and be on the same page with them. On the other side of our hearts, we were stiff and nervous. We were still worrying about our performances. After a few games, it was our turn to show what we had prepared. Our dance team was after the pantomime team, so we had little time to refresh our movements. Finally, we stepped onto the stage and showed everything we had prepared. I tried to smile as much as I could on the stage. Fortunately, there was no noticeable mistake. After all the performances, we ate Tanzanian lunch with people from town. The menu was something that seemed like fried meat rice. Honestly, this lunch was fabulous. I loved it. It was my first time being satisfied with the local food. After lunch, we had time to say goodbye to local people. We took a lot of pictures and videos with students and children. On the other side of school, my school's teachers took pictures of local families and printed them out for them. My friends and I taught them some dance moves, beatboxing, and clapping games. Modric was really good at beatboxing. He was indeed talented. He could replicate all the beats we showed him, and he could add something to them by himself. I was so sorry for his talent because his town is the only place where he can show it. He was a gentleman, too. When I was giving out my keyrings to children, I did not have enough, so I was hesitant to give them out or not. Then Modric told me to give it to girls instead of boys. I told the children that he was a real man. I encouraged him to go to the USA one day for his talent, and I promised him that I would support him one day. It was really our last time seeing the children. I will never forget the experiences and feelings they gave me. I will remember the girl who slept in my class. I will remember the moderator who showed me incredible talent. I will remember the best duo, Yummna and Shaiming. Bye, my friends in Tanzania. Bye, ninth night of Tanzania.

Day 10

. . . .

We woke up at 6 a.m. today and packed all our suitcases because we will move out of the island, Zanzibar, to go to the mainland, Arusha. Our volunteer work is all done! It is time for leisure now. We had our last breakfast at this hotel and rode on the bus. Then, the manager of this hotel followed us and stepped on the bus. He said, "It was all quality time while you were visiting. I wish for your safety for your rest of the trip. Thank you. God bless you." It was another thing that I could never think of happening in Korea. I am not sure about others, but I was really touched by his blessing. Yes, I agreed that I did complain about this hotel once. Maybe.. twice. However, when I have a flashback of my memories in the future, I would never think to have so many of these kinds of memories about a "hotel" in my life. For me, the hotel was just a place to rest. It wasn't anything special. However, this place made me realize that the hotel can be more than that. To be honest, I was more touched by his words than the rest of us because the hotel actually did one favor for me: they found my missing book. I did not want to be nagged by my teachers, so I asked them to check their lost and found box without letting my teachers know. However, they did more than that. They went to the room I stayed in and asked everyone for the missing book secretly, so my teacher would not recognize my mistake. I was actually really thankful for that. Honestly, I was at the edge of my ability to live with teachers. I don't want you to misunderstand this. My teachers did nothing wrong. They were nice and good people. However, their role as "teacher" had to be always on with us. It's not easy to express this burden... I mean...they have duties as a teacher. When I go to school, that duty ends after 4pm. However, that duty lasts for twenty four hours here. I got so sensitive even to the minor nagging on me as time went on. I even cried several times and Sophia and Luna had to always console me. Therefore, I really did not want the teacher to find out that I lost something and scold me. I was really thankful for them to understand me and help me out. I even gave them some tips before I left the hotel. My friends said I am crazy for giving them tips after all that happening of moving the rooms. Well…. I agreed with them for some parts. However, I always like to have a happy ending. So… why not..? I will never forget them. God bless them. The next destination for our bus was the house of the missionaries. The missionaries wanted to serve our lunch. I really like their Korean cuisines because I was getting sick of greasy food. After lunch and playing with the children, we left the house and hurried to the airport. We would miss our flight if the airport was as huge as Incheon airport. It was my first time feeling thankful for the small airport. After a short period of time sprinting, we finally got on the airplane. We actually had some stereotypes about small airplanes in Tanzania, such as it being a dangerous and uncomfortable airplane, but I actually had one of the best flights in my life. The plane was small, but I loved the ice cream they served, especially the strawberry flavor. After about an hour flight, we arrived in Arusha. Arusha wasn't like a typical country in Africa that people can think of. It was actually chilly. Then, we started our first tour in Arusha. First of all, we went to Art gallery. People can be like "Art gallery…?," but Tanzania actually has its own style of art, such as Tingatinga, so it is really important to see and feel the talent of Tanzanians. Again, I am not an art person. I don't plan to be an artist. However, art has been one of things that has inspired me for a long time. Plus, I like how I can be focused when I am working on art stuff. Visiting this art gallery was so expressive for me. I encountered a novel style of art that I've never seen in my life. I was surprised by the Tanzania baby girl's face looking at me. I felt like it was really staring at me. All the art pieces were really sophisticated. I would buy a small one if I got enough budget. For my next summer art exhibition, I will turn over a new leaf and follow their styles. After having quality time at the art gallery, we reached our next destination, which was our second hotel. Technically, it would be my third hotel room since I had an incident of moving the room at my first hotel. When we arrived at the hotel, the first impression that I got was.. "It looks like Smurfs' houses." All the rooms looked like mushrooms attached to the trees to me. It looked like we were the only ones staying here for now. I got saem room with Luna, but

Sophia got split from us. When I got the key to the room, I thought it looked like an ancient key from old cartoons. Luna and I climbed up the stairs and reached the second floor. Then, we inserted the key into the door's hole and tried to rotate it. However, something was weird. The door was locked very strongly. We did everything we could to open the doors. Eventually, we had to call a worker at this hotel. Well… she struggled a lot just like us to open the door, too. Anyway, when we finally entered the room, the first thing that came into my mind was that the "room is pretty dark." In the round room, there was a double-sized bed with one bedside table in the center. There was another main table and TV above it, but the TV seemed like it was not working. The left side of the wallpaper was kind of torn off. The bathroom was dark, too. The side wallpaper of the shower booth was torn off. Well… I would not say it is better than the last hotel, but I wasn't too stressed about the hotel because it was only for a night. When we unpacked our stuff and went out of the room, I faced the real problem. We were unable to unlock and lock the door since it is too old style. I called Mr. Adams. He struggled, but he did it. When we gathered for dinner, we found out other students' rooms were worse than ours. One of the students quit sleeping alone and decided to sleep with the teacher because he got too scared of the room. After dinner, I visited another girl's room and I was startled by the first scene I saw. I understood how better my room was compared to others. First, their lock system was too weak. Anyone could open the door even if they locked it, so they blocked the door with the chair. Second, the window was not completely covered and they were staying on the first floor. Third, their bathroom's light was out. Those three seemed to be the major problems. I worried about their safety. Honestly, I felt unsafe after looking around their room because we were the only foreigners around that area. You might think we overreacted. Then, Imagine being the only foreigner in the area you're staying and you are unable to lock the door and cover the windows. After looking at the condition of the hotel, I did not want to use this hotel water to wash my face and body. (Plus, only cold water was flowing.) It was time for me to use dry-shampoo that I brought. All the girls came to me and we shared it. I was so relieved to keep dry-shampoo for this day. After looking at another girl's room, I got a little bit frightened, just like Luna. We decided to fill our night with chit-chatting. Then, someone knocked on our door. I flinched, but it was my female teacher and Sophia. Unlike us, Sophia looked pretty sleepy. They were checking on the girls. Then, we suddenly started to chit-chat and explained our fear. That's where our long conversation began. No one got the idea of sleeping (except for Sophia), so Luna and I started to share our difficulties on this vision trip. I don't know where I got the boldness to be that honest with the teacher, but I told her how uncomfortable I am to be the only couple in this group and how I am at my edge of living with teachers. Fortunately, she understood me and talked to me. Even though we did not stay in the best hotel, I would stay in that hotel again if I could go back because I got emotionally consoled and stable after the night conversation with her. After she left our room with Sophia, we actually fell asleep right away. Maybe… it was because of a conversation with the teacher that made me emotionally stable. I think my first day of leisure was unexpected, but pretty good. Bye, my tenth night of Tanzania.

Day 11

. . . .

Today was the reason why I came to Tanzania. Our plan for today was to visit Tarangire National Park Tanzania. It was a safari place where we could meet wild animals. We came to Arusha because of this. We woke up super early and got on the Safari bus. The VP was on the same bus with us and he said it would take about two hours to get to our destination. The VP assured us to make a lot of memories on the way instead of sleeping, so we followed his order so strictly. We played all the games we knew very noisily for a full two hours. It was really hilarious when he said later it is now okay to sleep. Two hours flew by after playing all the games on the bus. My goal for today was not to see a lion or buffal, buto, but to see an elephant. The elephant was one of my favorite animals in the world and I had been so eager to see elephants since I was in Korea. Luna wanted to see a flamingo. Henry wanted to see the hippo. Sophia wanted to see the giraffe. The first animal we saw was a turtle, which was totally unexpected. When we went deeper and deeper into the park, I saw a scene from Lion King. No, it was even better. The endless meadow with birds flying in the blue sky and buffalos and wild boar wandering around was a speechless scene. The first person who got her wish came true was Sophia. After the guide heard the news of the appearance of giraffe, he turned the bus and hurried to the place where the giraffe was detected. It was super tall. It felt different from when I met the giraffe in the zoo. After seeing Sophia fulfilling her wish, Ibecame more became more desperate to see the elephants today. It didn't take long for my desperation to be solved. Our guides got reports about the appearance of elephants. We turned our bus again and I finally met the elephants. It was my first time seeing the elephants that close. I felt my reason to come to Tanzania being reached. Plus, the baby elephants were bigger than I expected and really cute. After the morning tour, it was time for lunch and we could have a buffet in the first of the scenery of endless meadows. About 10 menus were served and it was mainly curry. All of us really liked this meal. Rather than the foodRather than the food, the landscape grabbed more of my of my attention. I brought a cup of tea and had tea time with friends on the outside tables and chairs. It was the best tea I had in my life. After the lunch and tour, we left Tarangire National Park Tanzania and arrived at our accommodation. However, there was a huge problem for me. Eric started to feel sick. Shit. We assumed it was because of car sickness and believed that it would be gone after resting. However, I worried more and more because first, I am his girlfriend (obviously), and second, we are not in Korea. We are in a totally new country that we've never been to before. I decided to act more cautious and mature since there was a possibility of him getting more ill. Apart from my bf's sickness, the hotel was mind blowing. When we first entered the lobby, they served us hot towels with welcome mango juice with Tanzanian cookies. The lobby itself was too different from all the previous hotels we've been staying in. All windows were properly and completely closed with classy velvet curtains. There were huge fluffy sofas in the middle of the room. A minute after I arrived here, I really loved this place. Our room was close to Eric's and Henry's and it was far from the teacher's room. I loved it! On the way to my room, I saw a huge swimming pool and the hotel said it was open 24 hours. Of course, we immediately planned to spend all our hours there. My hotel room was spectacular. It had three king sized beds, a huge sofa, all completely closed windows, and even a FIREPLACE. On the other side of the room, there was a huge dressing table with a huge bathroom. OMG, there were even three nightgowns!?! Sophia, Luna and I felt like all our hard work was getting paid back now. That nasty hotel that we stayed last night made us more thankful for this current hotel. After we unpacked our stuff, we gathered in the dining room of the hotel for dinner. Our teachers said there isn't a specific schedule from now. All we had to do was rest, enjoy and gather at 6 am tomorrow for breakfast. Our dinner was a buffet and all different kinds of European meals were served. My boyfriend was not eating really well, so I got him some soup and hot tea. I assured him to take a good rest for today because tomorrow's schedule is quite tough. He agreed and he said it is okay for me to play in the swimming pool with other friends without him. I kind of felt bad for playing without him, but he said he will feel bad if I don't enjoy this place because of him. Therefore, after our wonderful dinner, we gathered at the swimming pool. On the way to the swimming pool, I made sure to put my boyfriend in the bed after a good shower. Except for my boyfriends and a few of our crew, most of my friends were there. This reminded me of Day 3. The only difference was we were in a better and bigger swimming pool. There were no other guests except for us in the swimming pool, so we could do whatever we wanted to do. I cannot exactly recall what we played in the swimming pool exactly, but I can recall the feelings that I felt at that time. It was nice. That's the best expression that I can give. I swimmed for 4 hours without the teacher's intervention. No wonder. The teacher's hotel room was so far from the swimming pool. They would not even have a clue of the time we dismissed. After we were dismissed, Sophia and I came back to our fascinating room and took a good quality shower. While Sophia was drying her hair, I put on a bonfire. (I actually put on the bonfire for the female teachers' room, too on the way back to the room.) I was glancing at others' Instagram and all of us put on the bonfire. When I was snoozing on the couch, after a short reading of the novel. (Well.. It was less than three pages long. I would not say that I read.) I relogged into my Instagram and texted my friends. They said we should get out of the room and look up at the sky. I woke up Sophia (I didn't touch Luna since she was super exhausted.) and brought her out of the room. Well…. I guessed we should have gone out of the room earlier. We couldn't find any stars in the sky. I looked at others' Instagram again. They were faster than us. They saw it. I kind of felt guilty for waking Sophia for nothing, but she said thanks for your attempt to show me stars. How generous of her. We came back to the room and fell asleep together on the nice huge double bed together. This day will be most memorable day of my life. Bye, my eleventh night of Tanzania.

As I wrap up this trip…

. . . .

"Asante Sana (Thank you)"

I still can't forget the smile of that child who looked at me while expressing gratitude.

I was born into a wealthy family, never lacking in love and attention from my parents, and went through adolescence just like everyone else. As I entered my teenage years, I started hearing a common question from those around me:

"What do you want to do in the future?"

My answer was always the same: **"I just want to get into a good university."**

I worked hard, but my life felt directionless—

drifting without meaning, hope, or purpose. Just as I began to question the meaning of my life, I came across a notice:

"Recruiting participants for the Tanzania Vision Trip."

My first reaction was: **"Tanzania...? Where is that?"**

With little interest, I did a quick search and found out that Tanzania is a country in East Africa. Even after learning that, I still only thought of it as a place I had seen in charity commercials on TV. Without any grand resolutions or deep intentions, I joined the **"2024 Tanzania Winter Break Vision Trip"** team out of curiosity, following a recommendation from my vice principal.

Our vision trip was planned as a two-week educational and volunteer program at **Hope School,** located on the island of **Zanzibar.** Shortly after joining the team, each of us chose an area of education we would focus on, and we began preparing. Traveling to a distant country to volunteer as a team required much more preparation than I had anticipated. From textbooks to teaching materials to lesson plans, we meticulously planned every detail to make the most of our short two weeks.

For two months, we prepared passionately as a team. The more we prepared, the more excited I became, not only for the trip but also for the bonds I was forming with my fellow volunteers. As the departure date approached, my parents, full of worry, bid an emotional farewell to their only daughter before sending me off at the airport gate.

After an exhausting **20+ hour** flight, we finally set foot in **Zanzibar**.

"This just feels like a trip to Southeast Asia..."

My first impression of Africa was that it wasn't as underdeveloped as I had expected. It actually reminded me of the tropical destinations I had frequently visited. The people there were not ignorant or threatening as some had warned me;

instead, they were as vibrant and lively as their bustling marketplaces.

The next day, after driving more than an hour on unpaved roads from **Zanzibar's city center,** we finally arrived at **Hope School.** As soon as we arrived, the local children stared at us with wide, curious eyes.

"Jambo! What's your name?"

Shyly, they didn't respond, only smiling as they looked at us. Leaving their silence behind, we quickly busied ourselves with lesson preparations.

Even as I prepared, I felt a sense of worry.

"If they're this shy, how are we going to have a proper class…?"

And just as I feared, most of the children entered the classroom stiff and hesitant. We struggled to lead the lesson, unsure of how to handle their quietness.

Then, I saw **her.**

A girl with big, bright eyes, a radiant smile, and a voice louder than anyone else's—her name was

Yumna. Unlike the other children, she answered all our questions in a loud, cheerful voice. Because of her, our nerves eased, and we were able to finish our first day of teaching successfully.

At the end of our long day, we sat on the steps, exhausted, watching Yumna playing with her friends. She laughed even louder than she had in class, running around with the biggest smile on her face.

"She doesn't have Barbie dolls or kitchen playsets, so what's making her so happy?"

I couldn't help but watch her.

"Yumna!"

Curious, we called out to her. Without hesitation, she ran into our arms as if we were already close friends. Seeing her bright smile, I picked a wildflower and placed it in her hair.

"Asante Sana (Thank you)"

She beamed even brighter, cherishing that small flower, later using it to play with her friends.

"It's just a random wildflower... can it really

make her this happy?"

I was stunned.

Watching Yumna smile so purely over something so small, I felt ashamed of myself. I had grown up in comfort, yet I had never truly been grateful or satisfied with my life. Even here, I saw discarded water bottles lying around and felt embarrassed by my own indifference.

Yumna and her friends, however, picked up what we considered **trash** and turned it into toys. That humbled me even further. I had always thought I was more knowledgeable, more experienced, and more privileged than them—but I failed to see the value in even a simple plastic bottle.

If I had been someone who only saw the vast **Indian Ocean,** Yumna was someone who saw the **shining seashells hidden within.**

Then came my third emotion: **pity.**

But ironically, it wasn't **them** I pitied.

It was **myself.**

They had the ability to find beauty in the smallest things, while I was the kind of person who overlooked the wildflowers right in front of me because I was too focused on the whole forest.

Thinking about all the **beautiful wildflowers I must have ignored in my life** filled me with regret.

As these emotions passed through me, the world around me started to feel **different.**

During our volunteer work, all I had felt was the **heat**—but suddenly, I noticed the **breeze** gently brushing against my ears.

"Ah… that feels nice."

It was such a subtle breeze, barely noticeable, yet for the first time, I felt gratitude for it.

And not just for the wind—I started appreciating all the little things I had never noticed before.

I want to make something clear:

I don't want to help improve their environment because I feel **sorry** for them.

I don't feel **pity** or **sympathy** toward them.

I simply wish for the world to **learn from them.**

I want people to realize how **arrogant and small we truly are.**

I want the world to learn how to **see things differently,** just like this once **conceited rich girl** did.

People who constantly search for **happiness,** drowning in their own desires, should ask these children:

"How do you float so effortlessly in your ocean?"

To **connect** them with the world, we need to improve their environment.

For their **wisdom and message** to reach others, they need support.

That's why I **couldn't just stand still.**

After returning to Korea, I began to ponder how I could connect them to my world. Then, a sudden thought struck me.

'Ah, I need to connect them with my friends first.'

It seemed to me that the most important task was to convey my friends' wisdom and aspirations to the future generation of talents. With this goal in mind, my friends who had traveled to Tanzania with me and I decided to establish a school club. These friends were the ones who had shared their hearts by preparing gifts for the children and local residents before our visit to Tanzania.

We gathered together and brainstormed the name for our club. Then, a word suddenly came to mind.

"Our club's name will be SOTZ, which stands for *Shout Out to Zanzibar!*"

The phrase shout out to does not simply mean to call out but is also used to express gratitude and respect towards someone. We chose this name to reflect that our club was not just about compassion and sympathy, but about showing respect and admiration for the country of Zanzibar.

As soon as we founded the club, we launched a website to share our stories. We began posting pictures we had taken with our friends in Tanzania, along with written stories. Through this, our schoolmates—though they had not personally visited Tanzania—were able to experience and connect with our journey and emotions indirectly. Furthermore, we used the website to share our club's activities, aiming to connect with even more people.

The biggest project of our club was the *Gift Project for Hope School Children.* To keep Tanzania in our hearts even after our vision trip, we organized monthly fundraising events at school for six months. Some were simple sales events, but the one that stood out to me the most was when we made and sold mandazi, a bread I had tasted in Tanzania. This event allowed our Cornerstone students to feel even more connected to the country of Tanzania.

Through six months of diligent fundraising, we were able to prepare 150 gifts. These gifts were planned and packaged by us using the funds we had raised. The gifts, sent during the summer, safely arrived at Hope School by ship around October.

Filled with this sense of fulfillment, I am now preparing to visit Tanzania again. During this visit, I plan to bring Christmas letters written by our school students to share the joy of Christmas with the children there.

I once lived without knowing my life's purpose or meaning, but through these experiences, I have come to realize them. My life's goal is to connect people.

Because of this, I aspire to become an international lawyer who listens to people's words and wisdom and connects them with one another. My ultimate dream and life's purpose are to continuously connect people and help them share their wisdom with each other.

Tanzania Journal

초판 1쇄 발행 2025. 3. 31.

지은이 서희원
펴낸이 김병호
펴낸곳 주식회사 바른북스

편집진행 황금주
디자인 김효나

등록 2019년 4월 3일 제2019-000040호
주소 서울시 성동구 연무장5길 9-16, 301호 (성수동2가, 블루스톤타워)
대표전화 070-7857-9719 | **경영지원** 02-3409-9719 | **팩스** 070-7610-9820

•바른북스는 여러분의 다양한 아이디어와 원고 투고를 설레는 마음으로 기다리고 있습니다.

이메일 barunbooks21@naver.com | **원고투고** barunbooks21@naver.com
홈페이지 www.barunbooks.com | **공식 블로그** blog.naver.com/barunbooks7
공식 포스트 post.naver.com/barunbooks7 | **페이스북** facebook.com/barunbooks7

ⓒ 서희원, 2025
ISBN 979-11-7263-286-1 03810

•파본이나 잘못된 책은 구입하신 곳에서 교환해드립니다.
•이 책은 저작권법에 따라 보호를 받는 저작물이므로 무단전재 및 복제를 금지하며,
 이 책 내용의 전부 및 일부를 이용하려면 반드시 저작권자와 도서출판 바른북스의 서면동의를 받아야 합니다.